MARTIAL ARTS

TAE KWON DO

David Amerland is second degree black belt in tae kwon do and a former British champion. The models are James Parr (second dan black belt), Tiffany Lin (first dan black belt and World Champion), and Brad Tombling (British and World Champion).

Special thanks to Shawn Strunsee (fourth degree black belt) for fact-checking assistance.

Please visit our web site at: **www.garethstevens.com**
For a free color catalog describing Gareth Stevens Publishing's
list of high-quality books and multimedia programs,
call 1-800-542-2595 (USA) or 1-800-387-3178 (Canada).
Gareth Stevens Publishing's fax: (414) 332-3567.

Library of Congress Cataloging-in-Publication Data

Amerland, David.
 Tae kwon do / David Amerland. — North American ed.
 p. cm. — (Martial arts)
 Includes bibliographical references and index.
 ISBN 0-8368-4195-6 (lib. bdg.)
 1. Tae kwon do—Juvenile literature. I. Title. II. Martial arts (Milwaukee, Wis.)
 GV1114.9.A44 2004
 796.815'3—dc22   2004045202

This North American edition first published in 2005 by
Gareth Stevens Publishing
A World Almanac Education Group Company
330 West Olive Street, Suite 100
Milwaukee, WI 53212 USA

Original edition © 2003 by David West Children's Books. First published in Great Britain
in 2003 by Raintree, Halley Court, Jordan Hill, Oxford OX2 8EJ, part of Harcourt Education.
Raintree is a registered trademark of Harcourt Education Ltd. This U.S. edition © 2005 by
Gareth Stevens, Inc. Additional end matter © 2005 by Gareth Stevens, Inc.

Photographer: Sylvio Dokov
David West editor: James Pickering
David West designer: Gary Jeffrey
Gareth Stevens editor: Alan Wachtel
Gareth Stevens designer: Steve Schraenkler
Gareth Stevens art direction: Tammy West
Gareth Stevens production: Jessica Morris

Photo Credits:
Abbreviations: (t) top, (m) middle, (b) bottom, (r) right, (l) left, (c) center

All photos by Sylvio Dokov except Getty Images: 15(br); Mike Hewitt/Allsport 6(b), 11(br); Adam Pretty/Allsport 16(b),
22–23; Matthew Stockman 19(br); Robert Cianfione/Allsport 21(br); Mark Dadswell/Allsport 24(tl).

Sylvio Dokov was born in Sofia, Bulgaria. For the past two decades, he has been one of Europe's leading martial arts
photographers. Sylvio works from his own studio in Telford, Shropshire.

Printed in the United States of America

1 2 3 4 5 6 7 8 9 08 07 06 05 04

MARTIAL ARTS

TAE KWON DO

David Amerland

GARETH STEVENS
GS
PUBLISHING
A World Almanac Education Group Company

CONTENTS

INTRODUCTION

Martial arts are ways of learning to defend yourself and develop physical and mental discipline. Many of them are also international competitive sports. Experts agree that the only way to really learn a martial art is to train with a qualified teacher.

This book introduces some of the basic techniques of tae kwon do, a popular martial art that comes from Korea. Read the text carefully and look closely at the pictures to see how to do some tae kwon do moves.

HISTORY

The Korean flag has both yin and yang and I-Ching symbols.

Tae kwon do, which was first developed in about 57 B.C., is over two thousand years old. Like most forms of unarmed combat, it was created by the people of its homeland, Korea, out of necessity. Originally known as *taek kyon*, tae kwon do was used for defense against wild animals but soon became part of the military training of young soldiers.

When tae kwon do was developed, Korea was divided into three kingdoms that were often at war with each other. After almost one thousand years of fighting, the Silla kingdom won the wars. Many soldiers of the Silla kingdom were members of an elite group called *hwa rang do*. Devoted to cultivating their minds and bodies to the highest level possible, this group practiced *taek kyon* and developed the honor code that forms the basis of tae kwon do.

This mural shows two warriors using taek kyon. *The mural is from the Koguryo period (about A.D. 400), and it is located at the Anak Tomb, in North Korea.*

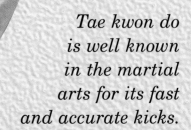

Tae kwon do is well known in the martial arts for its fast and accurate kicks.

TENETS OF TAE KWON DO

The philosophy of tae kwon do is based upon constant striving for excellence. The goal of tae kwon do is to become honorable and fit by developing five key characteristics.

The martial arts skills learned in tae kwon do are used to prevent conflict and violence, not to start them.

COURTESY: Courtesy to all those around us is a core principle of tae kwon do. Students must show respect to their instructors, to higher ranking students, and to all others.

INTEGRITY: One must be able to define right and wrong and have the conscience to feel remorse if wrong.

PERSEVERANCE: Nothing of any lasting value comes easily. If you fail the first time, or even the hundredth time, try again.

SELF-CONTROL: Tae kwon do students must control their actions and emotions both inside and outside the *dojang*.

INDOMITABLE SPIRIT: Never be afraid to be yourself and trust your judgment. Keep your ideals and your identity.

BELTS

The color of each tae kwon do belt has a meaning. It also stands for a rank. White is the lowest; black is the highest.

WHITE signifies innocence.
YELLOW signifies Earth.
GREEN signifies growth.
BLUE signifies heaven and upward development.
RED signifies danger, caution, and control.
BLACK signifies closure and the maturity of the student.

1   **2**

3   **4**

HOW TO TIE A BELT

1. Hold the belt with two-thirds of it on your right side.

2. Wrap the belt around your body twice, making sure that the second wrap covers the first.

3. Thread the right end of the belt behind both loops. Make a knot with the left end over the right end.

4. Tie the left end over the right end again.

CLOTHING AND EQUIPMENT

The two main styles of tae kwon do are ITF and WTF. ITF tae kwon do is a light contact fighting style, which encourages fast moves and multiple combinations. WTF tae kwon do uses powerful, straight kicks.

Basic clothing is similar in both main styles of tae kwon do. All students wear white uniforms, and black belts wear white suits with black trim.

1

2

3

In the International Tae Kwon Do Federation (ITF) style, competitors wear groin, mouth, and head guards, as well as hand and foot pads, but no chest protectors. The ITF scoring system rewards speed and good strategy, not sheer kicking power.

4

ITF
1. head guard
2. mouth guard
3. hand guard
4. groin guard
5. foot guard

5

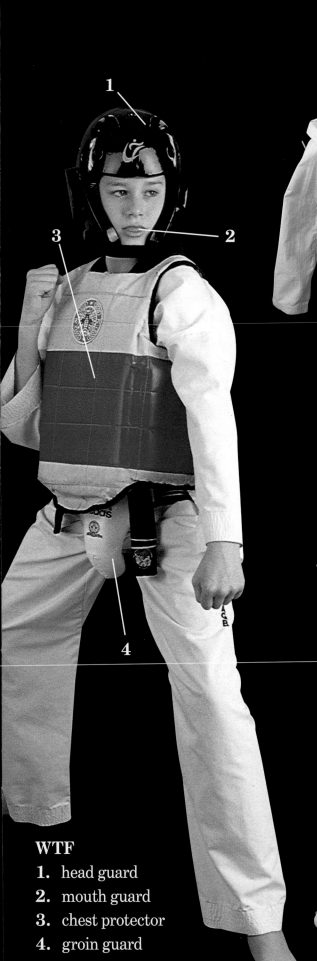

In the World Tae Kwon Do Federation (WTF) style of fighting, competitors wear head guards, chest protectors, groin guards, and mouth guards. Chest protectors allow WTF competitors to kick harder.

Because both styles of tae kwon do use fast kicks, the ITF and the WTF require competitors to wear either external or under-the-suit groin guards to protect against mistimed or badly aimed kicks that could cause serious injuries.

WARMING UP

In order to perform high kicks effectively, tae kwon do students spend a great deal of time warming up. They usually do stretching exercises with the help of a partner. These exercises focus on the hamstrings (tendons on the inside of the thighs) and the hip joints. Stretching partners need to communicate so that they push, but do not exceed, each other's limits.

WTF

1. head guard
2. mouth guard
3. chest protector
4. groin guard

FOREFIST PUNCH
(chirugi)

Tae kwon do uses two basic, straight-line punches: obverse and reverse. For obverse punches, the punching hand is on the same side as the lead leg. For reverse punches, the punching hand is on the opposite side of the lead leg.

Strike with just the knuckles of your index and middle fingers. This way, the power of your punch is focused on a small area. Punches focused on a small area are more powerful, much like a stream of water shooting through the narrow opening of a water pistol becomes more powerful.

OBVERSE PUNCH
Position the feet wide apart, with the lead leg bent slightly, and the body weight divided evenly between both feet. This foot position allows the hips to twist. In tae kwon do, the power of a punch comes from twisting the hips as the punch is about to hit its target. If your feet are not correctly set, you cannot twist to generate power.

REVERSE PUNCH

As with the obverse punch, position the feet wide apart, with the toes pointing forward. Hold the opposite hand drawn in to the waist. Punch with that hand, twisting the hips and upper body. The reverse punch permits the upper body to twist faster and further than the obverse punch. The result is more power.

Twisting the hips increases the power of a punch far beyond what the arm muscles alone could generate.

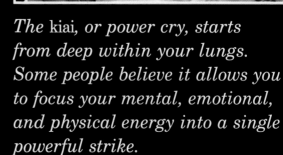

The kiai, *or power cry, starts from deep within your lungs. Some people believe it allows you to focus your mental, emotional, and physical energy into a single powerful strike.*

BACKFIST PUNCH
(dung joomuk)

The backfist is one of the most powerful, fluid, and effective punches in tae kwon do. The best way to think of it is as a backhand slap with a closed fist. A backfist punch reaches full power when the arm is fully extended.

The backfist should strike with the knuckles of the index and middle fingers.

BASIC BACKFIST

Cross your wrists at eye level with the backs of the hands toward you. Keep your striking arm on the outside, with the elbow pointing at the target.

Moving both hands at the same time, rapidly return the inside hand to the waist, palm facing upward. Push the outside hand out to strike.

REVERSE BACKFIST

The basic backfist can be improved with a little twist.

1. Face your opponent in a defensive position. Keep your arms up and put your body weight on your back leg. Bringing the back leg forward, step toward your opponent.

In competitions, the backfist is used at lightning speed. A backfist allows the competitor on the right to fully extend his shoulder and reach his opponent, who believes he is safely out of reach.

2 **3** **4**

2. Lift the back foot and begin turning your body in a circle, using the front leg as a pivot.

3. While lining up with your opponent again, cross your wrists as you would for a normal backfist.

4. Complete the backfist, striking the target. The reverse backfist gains power from turning the body.

KNIFEHAND STRIKE
(sonkal taerigi)

The knifehand strike is the tae kwon do version of the so-called "karate chop." It is primarily used to attack soft targets, such as the side of the neck and the throat. With special training over time, however, martial artists can make their hands tough enough to break wooden boards and bricks.

The striking area for the knifehand strike is the outside edge of the palm. This area has relatively few nerves. When the hand moves quickly, it can generate great power.

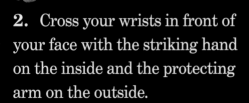

1. Start with the weight of the body distributed mostly on the back leg, with arms held at about chest level for protection.

2. Cross your wrists in front of your face with the striking hand on the inside and the protecting arm on the outside.

KNIFEHAND STRIKE IN COMBAT

Because of their speed and accuracy, knifehand strikes can be used in combat to attack targets that are difficult to hit, such as the base of the neck. Timing is vital when aiming a knifehand strike against a moving opponent. To maximize the impact, you should strike at the moment of an opponent's attack.

3

3. Pull the protecting arm to your waist, palm upward. The edge of the palm of the striking hand should travel to the target with the thumb tucked in to avoid injury.

A knifehand block uses a motion similar to a knifehand strike. The fighter on the left has blocked a kick with a knifehand block.

FRONT SNAP KICK
(ap chagi)

Most people have stronger legs than arms. In some cases, tae kwon do kicks allow a smaller, weaker person to defeat the attack of a stronger, bigger opponent.

1

In a correct front snap kick, the toes are bent back to prevent injury. The ball of the foot makes contact with the target. Focusing the kick on a small area increases its power.

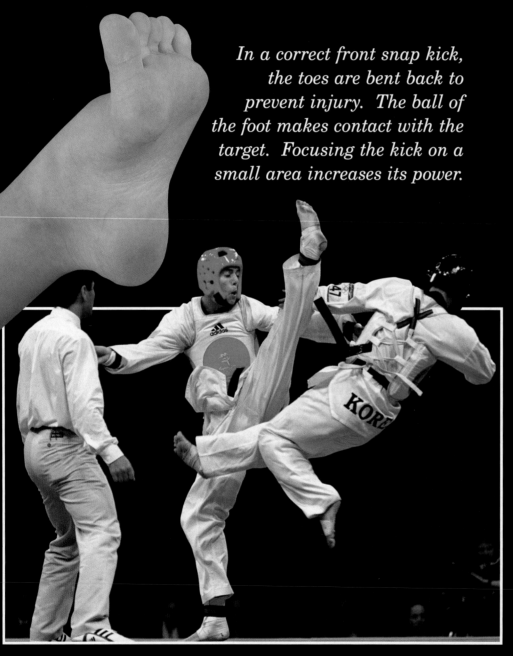

Spectacular kicks in competitions demonstrate the grace and power of tae kwon do.

1. Start with the hands up in a defensive position and the weight resting mostly on the back leg. Face in the direction that you will be kicking.

2 — **3**

The front snap kick is a very fast, powerful kick. Combined with a jump, it can be used to attack a very high target.

2. Shift the body weight entirely onto the back leg and bring the kicking leg into chamber position (off the ground, bent at a right angle). Point the knee at the target of the kick.

3. Quickly snap the foot in a straight line to hit the target. Keeping the toes bent back to avoid injury, strike with the ball of the foot. Pull the foot back into chamber position, then return to a defensive position.

ROUNDHOUSE KICK
(dollyo chagi)

A favorite of competition fighters, the roundhouse kick is executed by bending the knee to bring the foot up, then quickly whipping the foot around to strike a target.

1. Stand with your arms in a defensive position and your body weight resting mostly on the back leg.

2. Shift your body weight entirely to the back leg. Bend your knee to bring your front leg into the chamber position.

3. Extend your leg to strike the target. The striking area can be the instep or the ball of your foot. Pull your toes back to avoid injury.

FRONT VIEW

1

2

3

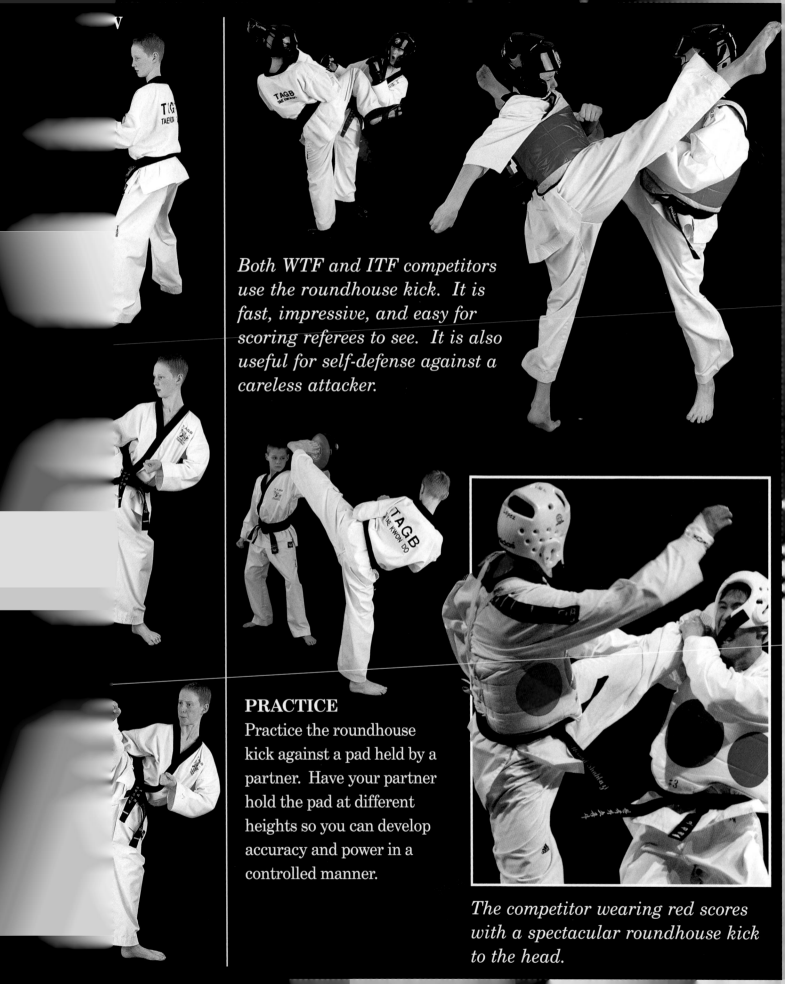

Both WTF and ITF competitors use the roundhouse kick. It is fast, impressive, and easy for scoring referees to see. It is also useful for self-defense against a careless attacker.

PRACTICE

Practice the roundhouse kick against a pad held by a partner. Have your partner hold the pad at different heights so you can develop accuracy and power in a controlled manner.

The competitor wearing red scores with a spectacular roundhouse kick to the head.

SIDE KICK
(yop chagi)

The side kick has serious stopping power. Even when used in light-contact situations, it can stop attackers in their tracks.

1

Using the side kick in competition is risky. It takes a long time for the kicker to recover balance when the kick does not hit its target, and this time can mean the difference between a win or a loss.

1. Start the kick by bringing your front leg up into chamber position. Turn your body sideways and raise your knee to the height of the target you intend to strike.

2 In the upper left corner.

The side kick can be aimed high. Its reach is seen here in a tae kwon do demonstration.

2. Extend your leg, using the outer edge of the foot to hit the target. Striking with the outer edge of the foot makes the side kick like a knifehand strike with the foot.

Nothing in tae kwon do matches the speed and stopping power of a correctly executed side kick.

HOOK KICK
(golcho chagi)

The hook kick is used mostly by ITF competition fighters. It is a fast, curving kick that is intended to strike the side of an opponent's head with the back of the heel.

Speed, good balance, and flexibility are critical in the correct execution of any kick, particularly when the move is used in a tae kwon do competition bout.

1. Like all tae kwon do kicks, the hook kick begins by cocking the kicking leg in chamber position.

2. While kicking, the foot of the supporting leg should turn away from the target, allowing the hip joint great range of movement.

TRAINING

Students of tae kwon do use a handheld pad as a target for practicing hook kicks. Controlled practice helps develop the speed, accuracy, flexibility, and balance that kicks aimed at high targets require.

3

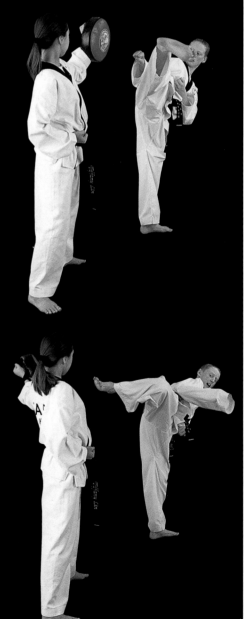

3. The movement of the hip joint increases the speed and power with which the kicking leg can be whipped at the target.

BACK KICK
(dwit chagi)

The back kick is known as a "stopping kick." It will stop just about any opponent you hit with it. Because of the power it generates, however, the back kick is probably one of the hardest kicks to control. It is best used for breaking objects and in competitions.

BACK KICK

1   **2**

1. Stand in a defensive position, with your weight mostly on the back leg.

2. Turn around on the front foot and look over your shoulder on the kicking-leg side.

A back kick can be used to check how an opponent will react to an attack. Any technique used as a check should not hit its target.

The back kick is the human equivalent of a donkey kick.

REVERSE SIDE KICK

In the reverse side kick, the kicker spins around and kicks with the back leg. This type of kick is closely related to the back kick.

1. Stand in a defensive position, with your weight mostly on the back leg.

2. Shift your body weight to the front leg. Spin counterclockwise on the leg bearing your weight until the back leg comes to the front.

3. Raise the kicking leg, keeping the knee parallel to the ground.

4. Extend the kicking leg, hitting the target with the edge of the foot.

3. Raise the kicking leg, keeping the knee pointed toward the ground.

4. Extend the kicking leg, connecting with the target. Point your toes toward the floor so that the heel of the foot makes contact with the target.

JUMPING KICK
(twimyo chagi)

Jumping kicks can reach high targets with great power. They require accuracy, speed, and flexibility and are among the most effective martial arts kicks. Their extra power comes from the momentum of the body jumping through the air.

JUMPING REVERSE HOOK KICK

1. Start with the hands in a defensive position and the weight of the body evenly distributed on the legs.

2. Bend the knees and jump up, spinning the body around in a counterclockwise direction.

3-4. As your back leg comes to the front, cock it into the chamber position.

5. Extend the kicking leg, striking the target as you land.

1

2

1

2

JUMPING BACK KICK

Some competitors think the jumping back kick is the perfect stopping kick for short-range matches.

1. With your weight evenly distributed on both legs, jump and spin to face away from your opponent.

2. Kick straight back before landing, making contact with your heel.

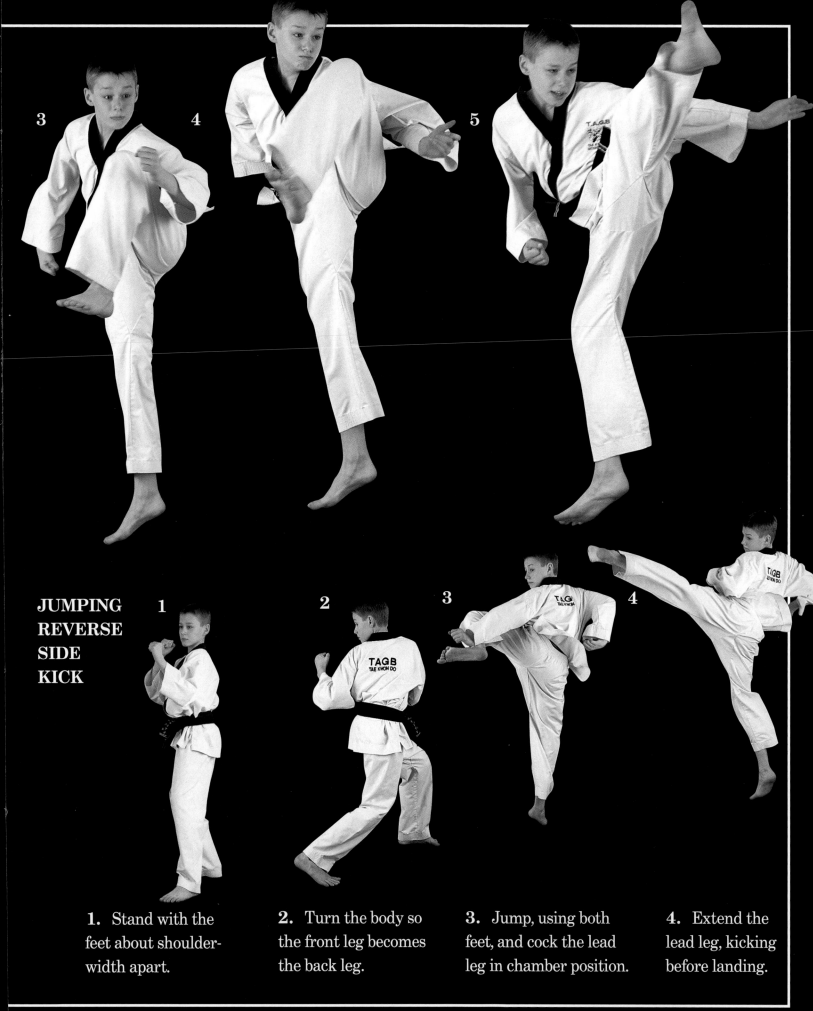

**JUMPING
REVERSE
SIDE
KICK**

1. Stand with the feet about shoulder-width apart.

2. Turn the body so the front leg becomes the back leg.

3. Jump, using both feet, and cock the lead leg in chamber position.

4. Extend the lead leg, kicking before landing.

SPARRING
(matsoki)

Free sparring is like unarmed combat. All sparring requires safety equipment and strict supervision. Sparring bouts in competitions are known as *gyoroogi*.

1

2

FREE SPARRING *(matsoki)*
1. A fighter wearing a blue dot and a fighter wearing a red dot square up against each other.

2. They change positions, looking for openings for attack.

SPARRING BOUT *(gyoroogi)*

1

2

3

1. Blue and red square up close to each other.

2. Blue bounces off red and attacks with a front snap kick.

3. Red anticipates the attack and counters with a roundhouse kick.

3. Blue sees red initiate a roundhouse kick attack.

4. Blue spins and counters with a reverse side kick.

4. Blue and red again square up close together.

5. Blue takes a step back, looking for an opening.

6. Red spots an opening first and uses a back kick to win.

USEFUL INFORMATION

Tae kwon do on the Web is every bit as intense as tae kwon do in the *dojang*.

United States Taekwondo Union
www.ustu.com

The World Taekwondo Federation (WTF)
www.wtf.org

The World Tae Kwon Do Headquarters
www.kukkiwon.or.kr/eng/

All of the Internet addresses (URLs) given in this book were valid at the time of going to press. Due to the dynamic nature of the Internet, however, some addresses may have changed, or sites may have ceased to exist since publication. While the author and publishers regret any inconvenience to readers, they can accept no responsibility for any Internet changes.

Useful addresses:
United States Taekwondo Union
One Olympic Plaza, Suite 104C
Colorado Springs, CO   80909
(719) 866-4632

World Tae Kwon Do Association
47 West 14th Street, 4th floor
New York, NY   10013
E-mail: webmaster@wtahq.com

The World Taekwondo Federation
Shinmunno Building, 5th floor
238 Shinmunno 1st-ga, Jongro-gu
Seoul, Korea 110-061
E-mail: wtf@united.co.kr

World Tae Kwon Do Headquarters
Kukkiwon, 635, Yoksam-dong, kangnam-ku,
Seoul 135-908, Korea

TAE KWON DO TERMS

ap chagi: front snap kick

bandae dollyo chagi: reverse roundhouse kick

bandae dollyo goro chagi: reverse hook kick

cha mom chagi: checking kick

chirugi: forefist punch

dojang: school or gymnasium used for tae kwon do

dollyo chagi: roundhouse kick

dung joomuk: backfist punch

dwit chagi: back kick

free sparring: simulated unarmed fighting

golcho: hooking

golcho chagi: hook kick

gyoroogi: competition sparring

hwa rang do: elite soldiers of the Silla kingdom who developed the honor code of tae kwon do

ibo matsoki: two-step sparring

ilbo matsoki: one-step sparring

jayoo matsoki: free sparring

junbi: ready position

kiai: yell that allows a person to focus mental, emotional, and physical energy into a strike

makgi: block

matsoki: sparring

nakka chagi: hook kick

sambo matsoki: three-step sparring

sonkal daebi: knifehand guarding

sonkal taerigi: knifehand strike

sonnal chigi: knifehand strike

sparring bout: a match within a competition that leads to scoring a point

taek kyon: the early name for tae kwon do

twimyo chagi: jumping kick

yop chagi: side kick

INDEX